MONOCHROME AND RAINBOW

MONOCHROME AND RAINBOW

PRATIK RAVINDRA KHANDAGALE

Hawakal
PUBLISHERS
New Delhi | Calcutta

HAWAKAL
New Delhi | Calcutta

HAWAKAL PUBLISHERS PRIVATE LIMITED
70 B/9 Amritpuri, East of Kailash, New Delhi 65
33/1/2 K B Sarani, Mall Road, Calcutta 80

Email info@hawakal.com
Website www.hawakal.com

Cover photo Shutterstock
Cover designed by Bitan Chakraborty

First edition May 2022

ISBN: 978-93-91431-68-6 (paperback)

Price: 350 INR | 14.99 USD

for
my family,
friends
and
all the readers of poetry

Acknowledgements

I have been writing poems for a long time now. Though I have self-published two poetry e-books before, I was mostly confined to posting my poems on various social media platforms.

I always dreamed about holding my poetry book in hand and reading the poems out loud. I am grateful to Kiriti Sengupta for giving me this opportunity and helping me to fulfil my dream.

I am also grateful to my mother and father for encouraging me to pursue my hobby of writing poetry. To my friends who helped me in curating this book, Thank you!

Contents

A LONG WAR

There is a long war I've been dragged into
Where I don't know who my enemy is
All I see around is different versions of me
Waiting to plunge onto each other
Some days, I keep on fighting endlessly
Some days, there is so much of stillness
That I can hear my own fear scream
Some days, I just sit cluelessly
Thinking if there is any hope for me
On such days when I am lost
I search for a way back home
But then again, I don't know where
Will it lead me to and whether the place
I'll finally go-to is my home or just
Another place which is waiting for a new war
to begin

A SHADOW OF AWARENESS

All along the road
I felt a hand touching me
But there was no one around
Quiet paths passing through the wilderness
And the canopy of the trees
Letting the sunlight peep through it
That was all I could see
The touch was familiar
As if I was in its presence before too
But this time it wasn't as lively as before
The hand quivered every time and tried to pull me back
It felt like it was frightened
Its grip was firm but couldn't stop me
I kept walking for hours till I reached a spot to rest
As soon as I sat down the hand touched me again
But this time I could see it
It was my own shadow
All along, it tried to talk to me just to hold me back
From treading a path that led to nowhere
I was walking into an uncharted area
That was filled with the illusions
I had created throughout my life
An area that covered misconceptions
With a coat that was a faux
An area where the truth disappeared
And where lies lived a royal life

My shadow disappeared again
But set the course of my journey
And this time, I got up and continued
To walk the same path
But with a flame in hand
To burn what was out there
And that flame was that of
Self-awareness

IN THE ABODE OF THE OTHER

It is wonderful and scary at the same time
To share your life with someone
To mingle with each other's angels
And sing lullabies to each other's demons
To pick up each other's habits
And mock each other's silly traits
To lament when the other is unhappy
Though you had a happy day
To dance when the other is cheerful
Though your mind went downhill the whole day
To spend sleepless nights with sleepy eyes trying to confront each other's nightmares
To cuddle up in each other's arms and walk through the glories of the dreams
To lose track of the days and nights
To finding it difficult to pass seconds in each other's presence

Why do we want to be with someone
and experience the spectrum of emotions
The similarities and polarities
The sharing, the caring
The attachments, the detachments
The love, the resentment
The flowers, the thorns

Is it just an adjustment
To escape the feeling of being alone
And the fear of being lonely all life long
Or is it the longing for being whole
And finding the missing parts of oneself
In the abode of the other

MY HEART IS A HAND GRENADE

Why do I seek the noise
And find it soothing
When silence is where
All the peace resides
Why do I yearn for love
That refuses to reciprocate
When I can be alone
And save myself
From being ripped apart
This urge to taste the extreme
Will burn me like never before
But then what's the point of
Not pulling out the chain
When my heart is just like
A hand grenade

WHAT AM I TO YOU

I am curious to know as to what
Do I look like to you
Am I the same person as I see myself
I feel that I am an iceberg
More beneath the skin than what
The outer body depicts
Am I a touch of high spirits
Or am I a washed out-self
Do I ignite the flames of intimacy in you
Or do I blow the nauseating ashes of detest
Am I a picturesque portrayal, a poetry
Or am I a fall of autumn, a random scribbling
Am I just a passing ripple of time, temporary
Or Am I someone who is meant to be held
Till we transcend to the other world

AN OUTLOOK TOWARDS LIFE

The subtle colours of the sunrise
The dense hues of the sunset
Captivate the eyes and enthrall the mind
It feels like the palette of a master
Working on a landscape painting
Where the yellows and reds
Are rolled out on the sky
It is celebrated, it is written about

The rest of the day
Is also brimming with colours
Pale, bright and gleaming with joy
But they are neglected like
An orphan child that wants to be welcomed
And they are chopped out from the reel
Unacknowledged

This abandonment of colours
Is similar to the outlook we have
Where only birth and death
Are etched as important and prime
But the life in between these two extremes is left unsung
And mugged from being serene and divine

A MISTAKE

I am addicted to listening to songs
And escape for sometime
From the hustle and bustle of life
Songs are a hypnotist taking charge
Of the mind, bending it in the direction
They want to, east, west, anywhere

But I have also committed a mistake
Though not a major one but certainly
A mistake!
I have associated you with songs
Mostly the happy happy ones

And now, my playlist that I had curated
Over the years is half empty
I deleted a few songs out of vitriolic anger
And the songs that still grace the list
Are untouched like the memorabilia
Frosted with dust in some corner of the attic

These songs are weighty
For me to handle and comprehend now
Even though I have thought
A hundred times to press the delete button
I always take a U-turn
Because these are the songs
Shared by you

AN ALLY, A GUIDE

I am an ally to all those
Strangers that feel dreary

I want to sit with them
Not as a therapist but as
a listener and hear them
speak about why they feel
like it's always a cyclone surrounding them
uprooting their happiness

I want to go on a ride
On the roller coaster of their emotions
Just to experience the twists and turns
The ups and downs
That they feel is punching them in the gut
Churning the guilt in their stomach

I want to watch the vivid evocation
Of the faintest incidents
In the cinema hall of their mind
To know exactly how and when
The inhuman dullness in them
Grew like a creeper and choked
The life out of them

I want to do this because I belonged
To their tribe before and
I have fought my way out of it
And as a former member of the tribe
I feel I am obligated to be a beacon
And guide them to an exit

REMEMBER ME WITH A CONDITION

If we part ways
And decide to never talk again
Would you remember me
And if you ever do, then please
Remember me when you beam with pleasure
And also, when you shed a tear
Remember me when the songs on which
We gelled once are being played around
Remember me when you drive through the city
And see people from the car window
Sitting by the sea being entertained
By the swelling and receding of the waves
Remember me when you pick up your
Phone to text or call someone
But don't remember me
If you ever feel loved someday
For I can be the reason
You'll question the feeling again

THE PARKING LOT

The parking lot of the mall
Is an underground safe house
For people trying to get to know each other
For you and me, it is a cocoon of ecstasy
It has been a witness to our amorous pursuits
And has also heard us say things that, if ever
are heard by anyone on the road
it could cause a traffic jam

the dim-lit interiors of our car
the soft fluffy comfortable seats
give a feeling of a presidential suite
of a five-star hotel

though we are engrossed in moving
our hands all over each other
through every crest and trough
our subconscious mind is alert

and praying that we remain
invisible to the people moving around
these quick escapes from the road
into the parking lots
is what we look out for
in times when we are so close
to each other yet a bit far
from our ultimate destiny
of a heavenly climax

INHERITANCE

This house was painted
With the sweat of my mother's sacrifices
The grass isn't green here anymore
And the walls speak the language of decay
But it still echoes the lullabies my mother
Used to sing to me
It still smells of the detergent that was
Used to rinse the clothes, it brings back the
Smells of yesterdays
I remember running around the house
Holding my mother's saree
And telling her all the happenings of the day
Some real, some made up
It was truly a place of abundance
Where my formative years
Were spent in the riches of life
Now, I need some time away from it
To disengage from the urge to
Sell it in return for a big house
I will come back someday
To this place but to
Only revive it from ruin
And pass it on to the new generation

I AM FORCED

I am forced
To carry my dead self
Just because it is in tune
With the norms of the society
I am forced
To be a person bereft of an identity
And float in mediocrity
I am forced
To become a voiceless pawn
And move squares according
To the ones sitting at the
Top of the power pyramid
This system stands tall like a gigantic
Skyscraper, the foundation of which
Are the remains of many like me
Who want to put up a fight

For their survival and dignity
But are bullied and subdued
By using dogmas that only
Cater to the hungry
Cannibals that feast on the human
Inside the body

Many a time these predators are disguised as our friends

I AM, I AM NOT

I am not hurt
When you did not text me yesterday
It is just that of all the messages
I received, your message was the one I was
Waiting for desperately

For when your name pops up on the screen
A volcano of contentment erupts in me
And my lips stretch as wide as the horizon
The leeches of thoughts sucking up my peace
Disappear suddenly elating my mood
And I drift into an imagination
Of a rosy world for the both of us

I am not hurt, ok, I am
For later in the evening
When I blew the candles
To cut the cake
I vowed to never text you again

ANSWERED PRAYERS

There is so much similarity between us
Right from believing in angel numbers
1111, 222, 333…
To texting each other right at the moment
We see them somewhere
Mostly we text at the exact same time
Though not on the same social media platforms

We are quick to understand when
One of us is going through a turmoil
Just a slight change in the pitch
Of the voice is enough to activate our radars

We overthink about the same situations
And then laugh our lungs out
When we share them the next day

Is this not what manifestation is all about
The gods we pray to have aligned with each other
And have sent us an answer to each other's prayers

Now it's up to us to change from being two strands
And weave ourselves into a single cloth of finest muslin

MONOTONY OF LIFE

I frequent a cafe with my friend
Sometimes twice, sometimes thrice in a week
We have a fixed place where we always sit
That lets us see the entire room
The barista brings two cappuccinos
Even before we get up to place the order
He likes us and has become our friend

There is a monotony to our life

While we sip the perfectly roasted arabica beans
We break into a chat about other people
We stare right into them to figure out
If they too are attached to strings
Like puppets and make movements
The way the puppeteer wants them to move
(let's say in this case the monotony)

Once the coffee has hit the right spots
We come back to talk about the both of us
It's mostly on career, finances and
Who will drive the car when we leave

My friend, she is well versed in astrology
And comes up with auspicious dates and time
To renovate our pale life
But in the end, disheartened,

she blames it on the mercury
In retrograde and goes back to sipping coffee

An hour later, we wave at the barista
walk out of the door
Look back inside again
And already visualize the both
Of us sitting in the same place
Continuing the legacy of our
Monotony

SAILS OF TIME

I know that the time
Has slipped away from my hand
That could've changed the course
Of my life
But the sails continue to drift me
In the same direction as before
Even though this path is stormy
I have lost the ability to steer myself
And I am adrift the rough waters
Hoping that someday the sea
Becomes calm
And the dark clouds make way
For some sunshine
So that I can look at the water
And see myself as a cheerful man
That has nothing to lose in life
But only win

BRIDGE OF WORDS

I know my words resonate
With your sinusoidal emotions
They are like messengers
Carrying a part of me
That has always wanted to be with you
Sing songs of other lands to you
Keep you warm in the cold
And sit in a garden with you on pleasant days
Admiring the nuances of nature
Though we are miles away
These words are a bridge between us
Just put a step forward from your end
You'll find me waiting for you
No matter how long it
Takes for us to be together

THE OLD WAYS

Now, when love is confined
To hashtags and selfies
That are devoid of any 'self'
Write to me like the old days
When every word was dipped
In feelings of oneness
When catching a glimpse of each other
In a crowded market was a priceless experience
And when a chance to merely hold hands
Brought the world to a
Standstill

WHAT IF IT COMES FROM WITHIN

In the minute of tranquility
My mind is at the loudest
Even the loudspeakers dare
Not compete with it
My ears have learned to
Shun voices from the outside
But I don't know what to do
When the voices I must stay away from
Come from within

AFRAID OF THE TRUTH

I am a pendulum
Swinging between days and nights
Being in the company of the sun and the moon
I do this continuously, every single day
For if I stop
I would have to meet myself
And that is one truth
I am afraid to face right now

IMPERFECTIONS

It's your perfection
That attracts me to you
But it's your imperfections
That lure me to stay
In them, I get a glimpse
Of your sublime nature
And how you use alchemy
To turn these shortcomings
Into gold that magnifies
Your ambience

DUALITY

There is a lot between us
Though it doesn't seem to be
But we are back to the point
Where we walked the opposite way
There is a lot to be expressed
There is a lot to be clarified
There is a lot to be felt again
There is a lot to be unfelt
And in this hour of
Doing and undoing
It is time for us to be observers
And witness this play of duality
So that we are cleansed of all the wrongs
That kept us apart

BEWILDERMENT

A dream is blooming in me
And I water it everyday
Though I want it to be lifeless
I have walked a great distance
Without you by my side
Always thinking about our
Blissful times
This dilemma is a roadblock
And I am stuck at the junction of bewilderment
There was a time when I had you
And no road can take me back again
The present is as false as all the promises
That never saw the light of the day
Should I keep on fighting
And trick myself into believing in a miracle
Or should I break all the illusions
And forget that I knew a person
Who vanished on the way

SHADOW AND THE SOUL

Between the shadow and the soul
There is some light that
Overpowers the darkness
This is a place where you
Reside in me
I am fond of this place
And I keep on revisiting it
Reminiscing the early times
Again and again to a point that
I forget that this isn't the reality
And 'we' no longer exist
And that it is only me now
Fooling myself into believing
That I am holding you between
My shadow and the soul

CROSSROADS

There is a person in me
That still wants the old pain
And hold onto the memories
Of the time when I was naive
And fell for words easily
Now when the seasons have changed
I feel like a lifeless person
Unhurt by any emotion
Any feeling, any event
The new love feels empty
barren and desireless
And the mind, it wanders
Aimlessly on new paths
But it always ends up at the crossroads
Of the old one

YOUR EYES ARE A STORYTELLER

I've read your eyes
The story they tell
Is filled with deception
Where the pain is hidden
Behind the expressions that are soothing
Every blink is like a new chapter
And the tears are like bookmarks
Attached to the pages where you
Lost faith in your own story
Your eyes show a craving
To find the perfect ending to the story
In which you though being the storyteller
Play the role of a side character

UNHEALED

I have been friends with anger
For a long time now
It has been my only companion
That refuses to leave me alone
But like the colours that become
Dull after ages and reveal the
Surface beneath it
Anger revealed itself to me
And it is nothing but
'Grief' that remained
Unhealed

PETALS, LOVE AND MATURITY

The petals are more mature
And know how to handle separation
They keep mum and put up a smile
Every time they are plucked from the flower
Just because someone out there
Is unsure about their love

A GLIMPSE OF DIVINITY

The place where I spent the last night
Nothing seemed familiar except you
I wish you take me with you
On journeys like these to such places
My life is livelier when I close my eyes
Than the one, I live in the day
For I can be with you holding your hand
Caressing your hair and just looking at you
Glow with radiance
It feels that the garb of the night suits us more as it
Brings us closer to each other
Your presence makes my fears run for their life
Your presence makes me a human I always longed to be
This journey with you also connects me with my soul
For in your presence, I get a glimpse of divinity

VIOLATIONS

Just a few seconds ago
A ceasefire was signed
Between the two quarrelling sides
Of me
And now, just a few seconds later
The ceasefire has
Already been violated

SUPERHERO

I am a superhero
With no face of its own
No fancy suits
And no cape
Just different masks
That change from
People to people
Beliefs to beliefs

ECHOES IN PRISON

Being trapped
In another person's prison
Felt like being sentenced
For crimes I never committed
But I endured the pain
For the prison felt
Like a heart that echoed
My name with every beat

ASSURANCES

I choose to walk away
Whenever they say that
"We are with you"
It's these assurances
That have robbed me
Of my true self
By invading my conscience
And tricking me to believe
That I am still free

ONE LAST TIME

I want to talk to you
One last time before I leave
Find me in between those lines
Whenever you'll miss me
Just close your eyes and
Feel the depth of whatever I've talked about
It will touch you in places
Where you've always loved to be touched
It will bring you so close to me
That you will feel my warm breath on your skin
And you'll also see yourself in it
In a way, you've always wanted to see
Raw, naked and stripped of all the lies
That you are forced to wear
And without any signs of
Shame and remorse

OPPONENT

Why is it that
Every time I win
I lose
Why is it that
Every time I lose
I win
And why is it that
Every time my opponent
Is you

MONOCHROME AND RAINBOW

After going through
All the shades of myself
I believed that humans
Come in monochrome
But then I met you
and in you, I could see
The rainbow

BACK ALLEYS

Suddenly all that felt
Like spring
Turned icy cold
The flowers wilted
Into clinkers of unfulfilled desires
All that glittered with life
Lost its luster

Suddenly I realized that
I am strolling through
The back alleys of
My mind

UNTIL YOU WERE GONE

I thought I knew you
Until the day you were gone
Unanswered questions still stick
Around and haunt the house
That was once lit by you
I doubt myself now
A lot more than ever
Did I understand you
Or did I misunderstand 'us'
I search for answers in the
Old conversations now
But I wake up with more questions
I wish nothing had ever happened between us
But I also wish that whatever happened
Would stay on forever

A GAME OF VIBES

In this enormous city
Cramped with fleshy skeletons
It is difficult to find
The one who we can say is 'mine'
It is because we are away from
Ourselves too
We just change in seconds
And try to match with the vibes
Of others who themselves
Are trying to match with
The vibes of someone else

SPIRITUAL APOCALYPSE

Your kiss on my forehead
Is a spiritual apocalypse
That aligns my deepest fears
With your warmth
This is an event
That breaks me to create me
An event that makes me yours
and then detaches me from myself

HEARTBREAK

It's a heartbreak
That wakes us up
From the worldly matters
And takes us back deep
Into our mind
Sometimes to forget
What we know about ourselves
And sometimes
To find out what is
Still classified

BROKEN BUT BEAUTIFUL

I keep seeking
All the broken things
Just to admire the beauty
Of what is left
After being torn into bits and pieces

Every piece resembles the
The same glory that
Once the 'whole' resembled

ONLY THING TO KEEP US ALIVE

In a world
Where we are labeled
Right from the moment
We are born
Let's drop all the guilt
And love each other
As if it's the only thing
That will keep us alive

AMIDST YOUR SOUL

I wish to slip like a drop
Of sweat on your curves
Treading a smooth path
Down to the origin of divinity
It is an expedition
I want to set myself on
to get entangled in you
so that I can completely forget myself
and wake up amidst your soul

PHOTOS – A MEASURE OF CHANGE

If you want to know
How much everything has
Changed between us
Just go through the photos
That rest somewhere in
An unnamed hidden folder on the laptop

The photos are in high definition
But the definition of our relation
Has blurred

IF I BECOME THE PATH

If I ever become
The path myself
Would you tread on it
Till the end
And meet me there

I would say that
This path could be a bumpy one
Having no straight roads
Having no warning signs displaying
The obstacles that lie ahead

But I would also say that
The destination would be the one
Which you've always wanted to be at
With me
A safe haven for the both of us

A PATIENT WAIT

The lies were what
I always loved
To put my faith in
And when the truth
Appeared at my doorstep
I took refuge in the
Back corner where there
Was no light
But the truth stood there
As firm as a deep-rooted tree
And waited for me patiently
To embrace it

IMPERFECT VAGABOND

To explore you
'Even today' is mystical
To not know you
'Even today' is a bliss
To search for your spirit
'Even today' is godlike
I always want to be your pilgrim
And be on a never-ending pilgrimage
For if I come to know you
The poetry would vanish
Love would die and all that is
Beautiful would wane
To know you would end my quest
And make my life perfect
But I have a wish
And that is to be
The imperfect vagabond

IGNORANCE

I could see myself
In your tears
That's the clearest reflection
Of myself, I had ever seen
It showed me
How loved I was once
And how my ignorance
Ruined it

A LITTLE REGRET

Let us click pictures
Whenever we are together
Years later, when we'll
Stand in front of the mirror
Looking at ourselves
And thinking about how far we've come
It will not show us the time
When we were mad in love
It will only show us two people
Staring at the mirror
With tons of thoughts in the mind
And a little regret hovering around

A HUGE VOID

Why does it feel like
An unfinished letter
Whenever I write about you
When the only emotion
I have in my mind
Is affection and care
The words I write have a profound meaning
Yet it feels that if they reach you
They would self-erase themselves
Creating a huge void

NOT THE REALITY

In the end
I am left with myself
After a long tiresome day
Of putting up with other people
This is the toughest part for me
As I am alone and
I find it difficult to accept myself
I've always seen me
Through the lens of my loved ones
And what I have always seen
Is my mistaken identity
An image that looks like me
But is in fact a reflection
Of all that I am not in reality

STRANGERS FOR LIVES TO COME

Let's fall in love for the night
And admire each other's moonlit face
Maybe we could find the treasure
We've been looking for
Or maybe we would see the grave
Maybe we would walk
Hand in hand the day after
Or disappear when the sun rises
And exist as strangers
For lives to come

NOT MY HOME

Just cling to me when it rains
And let me sink in you completely
That way, I would know
That you are not the one
To run away from me
In times of chaos
For I have been abandoned
By the ones who had promised
Me a home in them

CLOSER TO BEING ONE

I like the sound of my name
In your voice, whispered
when the intimacy
Between us is at the peak
And the heart has just skipped a beat
In anticipation of the next moment
That would take us
Closer to being 'one'

REALIZATION

Within a few days of knowing you
I realized that the universe had played
A part in uniting us at a time
When I had turned drab and grey
A few days with you
I lost the count of the times
I cursed myself for the disbelief
I had in the concept of companionship
Your presence is an oasis
Quenching my thirst in the sunny dessert
Of my own thoughts
Your presence is a portal
To a place where I can be myself
And see the world around me be
Joyful and euphoric

DEATH OF EGO

Return to me
Like a sealed envelop
That has a blank paper in it
I will fill it with new words
And add a new meaning to 'us'
And re-write the tales
With an ending that
Starts at the death of
Ego

THE TERROR WITHIN

I cannot sugarcoat my pain
And pretend to be happy
When there is a rage
Brewing in me
So, I opt for reticence
And the night so that
No one can hear me
And see me unleash
The terror within

LOST IN CONFUSION

In the evening
I wish to be with you
With the setting sun
In the backdrop
My delusions go far away
Beyond the sea
And what remains is love
That laughs and dances

When I see you walking towards me
I become a curious child
That believes in miracles
And thrives on hope
The same hope
That has kept us afloat
When all was believed to have
Been lost in confusion

SHIVERING IN SILENCE

Silently
I am searching for a hand to hold
To defrost my frozen aura
But every hand that I touch
Reminds me of you
And then I move away
Shivering in silence

TIME – THE CUPID

Let time play the role
Of the cupid
Till then let us declutter
and empty ourselves
of all the weeds of pessimism
that have grown over the years
For it's the emptiness
That will attract the arrows

A BOND FOR ETERNITY

You are far from me
This reason is enough
For me to think about you all the time
Few hours of talking to you
Feels like a lifetime
I guess, we were destined to cross
Each other's paths so that
We could embark on the holy grail of love
And spread its seeds all around
Let this distance between us
Be a reminder that a separation
Of a few kilometers is not a hindrance
But a temporary mismatch of fate

I am sending my love through
The winds that blow from my place to yours
Let them pass through you
You have become the talk
Of every single cell of my body
I am waiting for the day to arrive
When you to come to me
And seal a bond for eternity

A FALSE INTERPRETATION

Every second feels perpetual
When my eyes are glued to the watch
Waiting for the time to come
When you would talk to me again
For I am caught in a web of lies
As I interpreted the meaning of silence
The way that pleased my mind

A SOLUTION

I know there is something
Wonderful between us
But the uncertainty
Of the days to come
Is a barricade blocking me
From diving deep into you
As I fear it would
Lead to a moment
Where walking away from each other
Would be the only solution
To keep our love alive

UNVEIL THE SCARS

Do not hide from me
Let your scars unveil the agony
Of loving someone too much
I have saved myself
Keeping you in my mind
But to see you tremble now
Is like going back in time
And living the life
That shook me to the core

RESTLESS PEACE

You pull me like a magnet
But I don't know whether I should
Make an ingress or walk backwards
Though my feet are clear
Of any stains of my former self
And I have long left my vulnerability
On the sidelines
I still hang back from being with you
For your peace is pristine
But my peace is still restless

MORE THAN EVER

Show me that side of you
Which you have never revealed
And are frightened to confront
I want to see how damaged you are
Though you seem to be cheerful
All the time floating around
With a smile on your face

I do not claim to be a healer
To heal you from any suffering
But I promise you
Irrespective of what I get to see
I will love you more than ever

UNCONDITIONAL

The river carries with it
The water of lost dreams
Meandering through the wild
Unknown about its path
But the sea never questions
The river and embraces it
Like a lover, sometimes in the presence
Of the light
And sometimes in the darkness
Of its own fallen angels

A BAGGAGE OF MEMORIES

When the gate opened
I stood there in front of it
Hesitating to enter inside
I was
Afraid, that I would be loved again
In the same way as before
Afraid, that I would be hearing
The same words again
Afraid, that I would be a part
Of something temporary
Afraid, that if this new love
Turns out to be real
I would lose what I've been
Carrying with me
A baggage that holds
The memories of you

LYRICS OF FREEDOM

The lyrics of life make sense now
When I sit by the window
Searching for freedom
In the vast open sky
In the globetrotting birds
The chains I am locked up in
Are invisible and the cage
Is my own house
I can see my mind crumble
And thoughts become a burden

The lyrics make sense now
When all I can do is wait
And let the days pass
Till I get my freedom back